D1525727

Iosepho suo
Theodoricus

TONIGHT THEY ALL DANCE

Tonight They All Dance

92 LATIN & ENGLISH HAIKU

Edited by
Dirk Sacré & Marcel Smets

English Translations by
Herman Servotte

Illustrations by
Mark McIntyre

BOLCHAZY-CARDUCCI PUBLISHERS, INC.
WAUCONDA, ILLINOIS

This publication was made possible by

PEGASUS LIMITED

Laurie K. Haight
General Editor

Georgine S. Cooper
Allan Kershaw
Contributing Editors

Robert Emmet Meagher
Layout and Design

Copyright ©1999
Bolchazy-Carducci Publishers, Inc., USA
All Rights Reserved
Illustrations copyright ©1999 Mark McIntyre

ISBN 0-86516-441-X hardbound
ISBN 0-86516-440-1 paperback

Published by
Bolchazy-Carducci Publishers, Inc.
1000 Brown Street
Wauconda, Illinois 60084

Library of Congress Cataloging-in-Publication Data

Tonight they all dance : 92 Latin & English haiku / edited by Dirk Sacre & Marcel Smets ; English translations by Herman Servotte ; calligraphic drawings by Mark McIntyre.
p. cm.
Includes bibliographical references.
ISBN 0-86516-441-X (alk. paper)
ISBN 0-86516-440-1 (pbk. : alk. paper)
1. Haiku, Latin (Medieval and modern)--Belgium--Translations into English. 2. Haiku, Latin (Medieval and modern)--Beligum. I. Sacre, Dirk. II. Smets, Marcel, 1925- III. Servotte, Herman, 1929-
PA8164 .T58 1999
874'.0408--dc21 99-21620
CIP

Table of Contents

Foreword

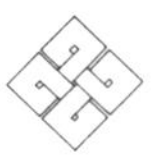

Tonight They All Dance contains poems written by Harundine, a Belgian group of Latin haiku poets: Hilda Borremans [H.B]; Renil Cappelle [R.C.]; Hugo Kempeneers [H.K.]; Dirk Sacré [D.S.]; Gillis Sacré [G.S.]; Marcel Smets, president [M.S.]; Leo Vander Elst [L.V.]; Anne Vermylen [A.V.]; and Andries Welkenhuysen [A.W.]. The English translations, by Herman Servotte, are not meant to be literal but rather to be poetic. The Introduction was written by Marcel Smets and Andries Welkenhuysen; it was translated into English by Herman Servotte. The vocabulary was added by Dirk Sacré. The final editing was done by Dirk Sacré and Marcel Smets.

The origin of the haikus is threefold: some are adaptations from classical, both Greek and Latin, verses, from Sappho to Martial; other ones are Latin translations of Japanese haikus; finally, a large number consists of new Latin creations.

In the Endnotes to this volume, each Haiku is followed by a reference, often abbreviated. Thus Mart. - L.V. means that a verse of Martial has been turned into a haiku by Leo Vander Elst; M.S. - A.W., that a Dutch haiku of Marcel Smets has been translated into Latin by Andries Welkenhuysen; An Michiels - Har., that a Dutch or a Latin haiku of the student An Michiels has been either translated into Latin or adapted by the members of Harundine; A.V., that the haiku is an original Latin poem of Anne Vermylen. For the benefit of readers who are still learning Latin or whose Latin is too far behind them, we have added notes and a complete vocabulary.

Introduction

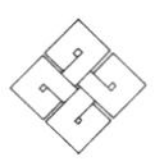

To write a haiku, a poem as short as one breath, seventeen syllables spread over three lines, is something of a game, somewhat like Scrabble™. Its content is equally ordinary, matter of fact, often playful: an apparently insignificant moment in nature or a seemingly trivial happening is observed with empathy (in this case one also speaks of a *senryû*, i.e. a haiku-type satiric/humorous poem on a human subject) and offered to the reader without comment. A haiku sees directly, without comparisons and almost without metaphors; it touches things in the stillness of the mind, trees in the rain, an autumn leaf that falls, a small child carrying a huge loaf; trivial events indeed, but which, when looked at in silent contemplation, open vistas of deep significance. The French poet and translator Philippe Jaccottet rightly observes that in a successful haiku "infinite space opens itself from almost nothing." This "almost nothing" asks for an unadorned vocabulary, which is hardly literary and remains simple, without self-centered concerns.

The haiku is a typically Japanese artform. It is more than four hundred years old; since the beginning of this century it has acquired worldwide significance. Almost every Western literature has its haiku poets, its centers and its periodicals for the practice of the haiku. In Flanders Bart Mesotten, a classicist and a theologian, has been an enthusiastic and inspiring "haikuist." As an example of his skill we quote a haiku from the collection *Day, Light* (1980), which was translated into Latin by one of his former fellow students:

Porta praeclusa tamen intrat formica non incurvata.	Though the door is closed, the ant comes in. without bending down.

Other classicists have tried their hands at writing Latin haikus. In Germany the philosopher and theologian Heinrich Reinhardt (b.1947) has already published three collections of "haicua" and the latinist Anne-Ilse Radke (b.1940) has recently given us another collection. In France Geneviève Immè published only a couple of months ago a collection of 365 haiku poems, one for every day of the year. In Belgium Marcel Smets, a classicist and retired teacher, took the initiative that led to the formation in March 1995 of a Flemish Association for Latin Haikus. Its name, Harundine, refers to the humble reed that, according to Bucolics 6.8, could be used by Vergil's shepherds to try out their ditties. Since then some teachers and professors of Latin together with one student have regularly convened under the chairmanship of Marcel Smets to discuss, to improve, and to enjoy their work. The school teachers among them also contribute haikus of their pupils. Some of these are surprisingly beautiful, and they need no correction, but in most cases these haikus merit revision.

The Latin language lends itself readily to chiseling formally correct haikus. The best-known Latin meter, the hexameter, in its pure dactylic form, consists of exactly seventeen syllables. One is reminded here of the famous line from Vergil's *Aeneid*, *Quadripedante putrem sonitu quatit ungula campum* (8.596), "the drumming of the horses' hooves shakes the sandy plain." This can be rewritten in three short lines, and one obtains, formally at least, a haiku:

Quadripedante
putrem sonitu quatit
ungula campum.

Other hexameters can, with a slight alteration, be turned into haikus. The Vergilian *Aret ager; vitio moriens sitit aeris herba*, "The field is parched, the grass is athirst, dying in the tainted air" (*Bucolics*, 7.57) can be rewritten as follows:

Arescit ager,
vitio sitit aurae
moriens herba.

Obviously a hexameter, even if it consists of seventeen syllables, is not a haiku. But a poem like Vergil's *Georgics* contains many passages that evince a remarkable similarity to the haiku, especially when they use one of the "season-words" that are so characteristic of the genre. What we want to show with these examples is how easily the technique of the haiku can be used in Latin, the more so as the haiku is a syllabic verse-form that is not tied up with metrical schemes. There is no need, therefore, to consult handbooks of ancient prosody: there are no binding metrical rules. Taste and a certain familiarity with the poetical stylistics of Latin are all that are required for building a graceful tristichon.

As a matter of fact some rhythmical cadences seem to present themselves. The short lines 1 and 3 of the haiku are tailor-made for the adonic scheme (úngula cámpum, móriens hérba, etc.). However, as this cadence rapidly hardens into a monotonous drone, one should use it with care to obtain a poetic effect.

As a language Latin is certainly not less suited for the haiku than our modern Western languages. Its density of expression manifests itself in the absence of articles and in its sparing use of prepositions, pronouns, auxiliaries, and conjunctions. Some people object that Latin is ill-suited for haikus because of its alleged limited vocabulary. Do Latin words exist for things, animals, plants of our daily observation? The answer is loud and clear: of course they do exist. One does not come across these words when reading the war reports of Caesar or the orations of Cicero. But in Vergil's *Bucolics* and *Georgics*, Ovid's *Metamorphoses*, Phaedrus' fables, Pliny's encyclopedia, and numerous other works one finds tables and chairs, hammer and anvil, linnet and crow, ant and worm, willow and elderberry, and lots of words, enough to describe our concrete and physical observations.

What is more, Latin's rich variety of shades of meaning in words chosen, and its flexibility of word order give it an advantage over modern languages. For one who likes Latin and the poetical play with words, hammering out a haiku is a real pleasure, and even secondary school students like to build haikus, often with satisfactory results, as we have often witnessed ourselves.

For the beginner we should like to add some advice. The first advice is to avoid elisions and the use of hiatus, for they cause confusion and even irritation; the second advice is to respect the 5-7-5 rule, for if one doesn't, one will never experience the bracing effects of the struggle with self-imposed limits. Old hands, who have shown their ability to write correct haikus, can of course transgress these limits and write haikus in free style. We hope this book will give pleasure to many and incite young and old, teachers and pupils to read and to try their hands at the writing of haikus.

CAELESTIA

I

In a reddish glow
the evening sun is about
to leave the still earth.

II

Together they watch
the far away Pleiades,
a husband and wife.

I

Sol vespertinus
rutilanti nitore
terram relinquit.

II

Mirantur una
Pleïadas remotas
coniuges ambo.

III

In thousands of panes
there flows an ocean of clouds—
darkness its splendour.

IV

An oppressive fog,
and the weak sun errs moonlike
among the dark trees.

III

In mille vitris
oceanus nimborum
fluctuat splendens.

IV

Iners nebula,
sol velut luna vagus
arbores inter.

一

V

Oblitus est fur
in fenestrula mea
lunam splendentem.

The burglar forgot
what stood high in my window:
the glimmering moon.

VI

Umbram virgulae
nitor Hispaniensis
reddit piceam.

Spain's punishing sun
turns the shadow of a twig
into pitch-black jet.

VII

A moment's sunshine
and all the wet cars begin
to sparkle and flash.

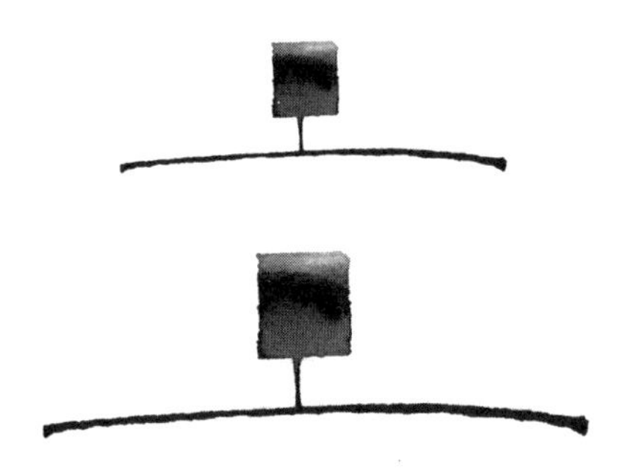

VIII

Red colours the sky,
and silence invades the earth:
night is near at hand.

IX

A leaden gray sky
weighs heavily on the poor
under its cover.

VII

Sol modo fulsit,
umentes ecce raedae
nitescunt omnes.

VIII

Rubescunt caeli,
terrae silescit murmur,
cuncta noctescunt.

IX

Incanum caelum
opprimit operculo
homuncionem.

—

X

Aurora sacra
pedetemptim penetrat
terram polumque.

The sacred morning
penetrates the earth and sky,
moving step by step.

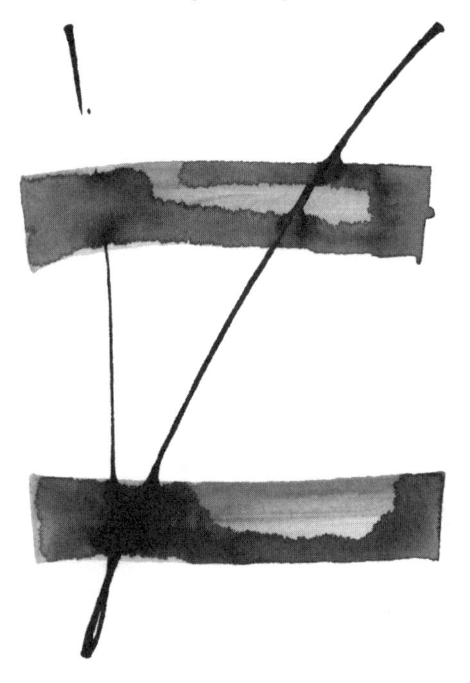

TERRESTRIA

XI

All through the night I
have not said a single word:
the waves are seething.

XII

Droplets of rain glide
softly along the branches
like the dew of dawn.

XI

Per totam noctem
non unum dixi verbum;
aestuant fluctus.

XII

Stillae per ramos
delabuntur leniter
et quies rorat.

XV

Dead leaves feed the fire;
hundreds of stars leap upwards
crackling in the dark.

XIII

Glebas iacentes
aestas pulverulenta
solibus coquit.

The dusty summer
with its manifold suns bakes
the clods of brown clay.

XIV

Silent salices
dum faber nebulosus
clavos percutit.

The willows keep still
as the workman wrapped in mist
hammers in his nails.

XV

Emicant stellae
mortua dum folia
consumit ignis.

XVI

Trunco mortuo
fagi nuper decisae
merula canit.

On the lifeless trunk
of the newly felled beech-tree
a blackbird's singing.

XVII

Cogitabunda
diu, tandem decidit
unica gutta.

Taking time to think
at last it falls from the branch,
this lonely droplet.

XVIII

Superbit flava
inter herbas aphaca,
cras evanescet.

The dandelion
proudly rears its yellow head
and will soon be dead.

XIX

First day of autumn:
motionless a ladder leans
against the plum tree.

XX

The fountains tinkle
and water lilies doze in
the old people's home.

XXI

At the field's far end
a flower falls suddenly
cut off by the plough.

XXII

At the field's far end
a flower has been hit by
a plough passing by.

XIX

Autumno primo
sub pruno restant scalae
stantque quietae.

XX

Aquae saliunt
dum dormiunt nymphaeae
in horto senum.

XXI

Ultimi prati
flos decidit ilico
tactus aratro.

XXII

Ultimi prati
flos tangitur aratro
praetereunti.

XXIII

The October rose:
soon after sunrise upright
now slightly drooping.

XXIV

Gods I do not know
but only these chamomiles
shining in the night.

XXV

The light stubbles are
about to catch fire and to
burn with crackling flames.

XXIII

Erecta mane
nunc paululum demissa
Octobris rosa.

XXIV

Deos non novi,
has tantum chamomillas
nocte lucentes.

XXV

Levem stipulam
crepitantibus flammis
urere coepit.

XXVI

Laurus accrescit
fluminis prope ripam
scopulos inter.

The laurel tree grows
near the banks of the river
among the dry rocks.

ANIMALIA

XXVII

Nidulus tepet:
pipilat avicula
os et apparet.

Its nest is lukewarm;
the small bird chirrups, its beak
becomes visible.

XXVIII

Dum spatiatur
pedes tollit ardea
quasi foedentur.

The stalking heron
lifts his feet as if they had
been sullied in mire.

XXIX

The cicada's song
will rarely tell you how near
on your heels is death.

XXX

In his cage the bird
warbles cheerfully as he
hops from branch to branch.

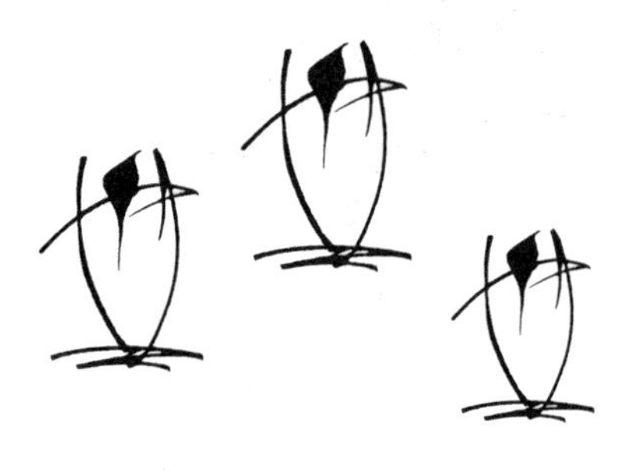

XXXI

A dreary headache and
in the distance I can hear
the birds chirruping.

XXIX

Vix cicadarum
intellegis e cantu
quam mors festinet.

XXX

Intra caveam
mite salit et canit
avis lasciva.

XXXI

Levi dolore
capitis aviculas
procul audio.

XXXII

It's pouring with rain;
a lone swallow darts screeching
across the still lakes.

XXXIII

Motionless amid
the immense and stubbled fields
the blue heron stands.

XXXII

Ruit pluvia;
stridens hirundo lacus
circumvolitat.

XXXIII

Immensas inter
stipulas ardea stat
neque movetur.

XXXIV

In nemoribus
cuculi vox auditur
semper remota.

In woods the cuckoo's
call is often to be heard
but always distant.

XXXV

In vitro lente
gyrat piscis, regyrat
pellucidulo.

In a glass fishbowl
a sluggish fish turns and turns
about in the light.

XXXVI

Feles annosa,
circum dum saltant mures,
dormit quieta.

The elderly cat
sleeps peacefully; all around
the mice are dancing.

XXXVII

Hearing the couple
quarrel, the tomcat lies down
on the garden wall.

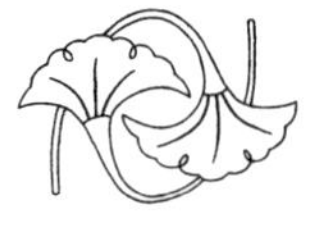

XXXVIII

The tremulous mouse
hangs in the mouth of the cat:
precious cruel spoil.

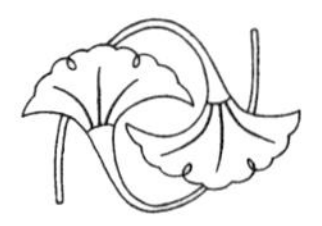

XXXIX

With elegant ease
the cat jumps up from dense grass
pouncing on a bird.

XXXVII

Illa dum saevit
in illum, catus audit
sedens in tecto.

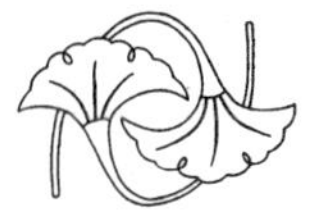

XXXVIII

Inhaeret arcte
felis ori tremulus
mus praeda saevae.

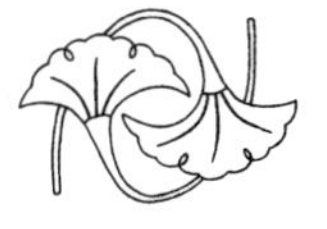

XXXIX

Ex herba densa
saltu prosilit leni
feles in avem.

XL

When the black cat comes
stealing unseen through the grass
her green eyes come first.

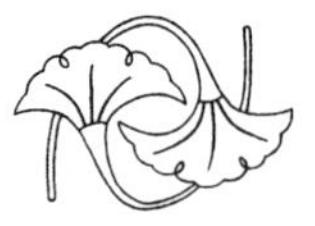

XLI

As the pumice rocks
keep falling, the little dog
lies hiding his fear.

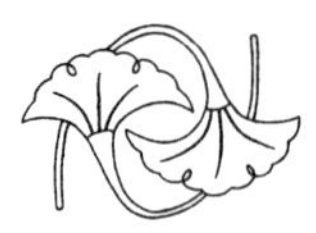

XLII

Two donkeys stand by
the olive tree, their small hooves
are white with the dust.

XL

Adrepit feles
nigra, praecedentibus
oculis glaucis.

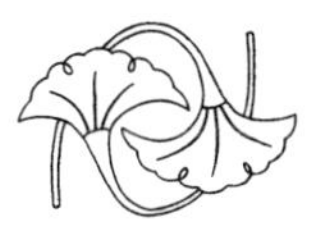

XLI

Anxia iacens
latet canicula dum
pumices cadunt.

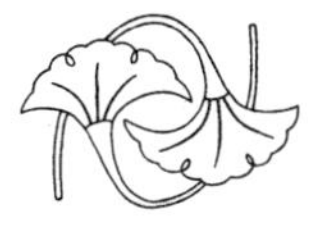

XLII

Aselli duo
pedibus pulveratis
stant sub oliva.

三

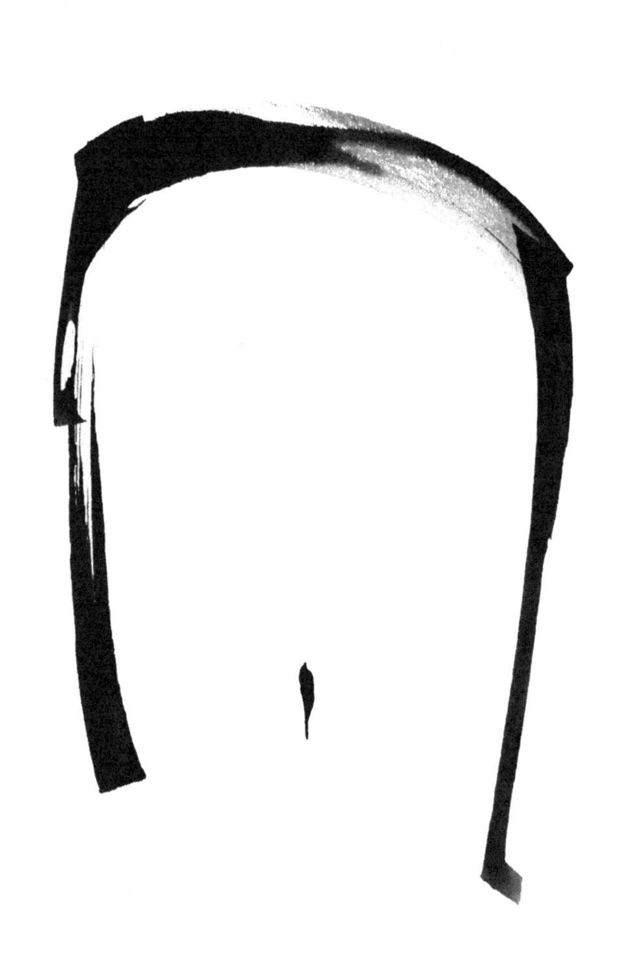

XLIII

Plangit asinus
miseram vitam suam
solus in prato.

The donkey alone
in the wide meadow laments
his life's loneliness.

XLIV

Angustum terens
iter, extulit ova
formica cauta.

The diligent ant
goes its own hard way and brings
the eggs safely home.

XLV

Araneola
perspicillo suspensa
circumvolitat.

The tiny spider
has got hold of my glasses
and dances ahead.

XLVI

Oh the small old pond!
A frog has jumped from its bank
and the waters clang.

XLVII

On his porch at dusk
the elderly man watches
the leap of the frog.

XLVI

O vetus stagnum!
Rana de ripa salit
ac sonant aquae.

XLVII

Senex in xysto
sub vesperum percipit
ranam saltantem.

☰

XLVIII

Hircus proterve
arietat stabulum
cornibus suis.

Brutally the buck
batters the strong stable walls
with heavy antlers.

XLIX

Quando non dormit
terret animalia
leo rugiens.

When he's not asleep
the lion's roar terrifies
all the animals

L

In colle sedet
auriculis arrectis
lepus immotus.

On the mountainside
the hare sits up motionless,
now he is all ears.

LI

Hic iacet serus
gramine papilio
gelu deprensus.

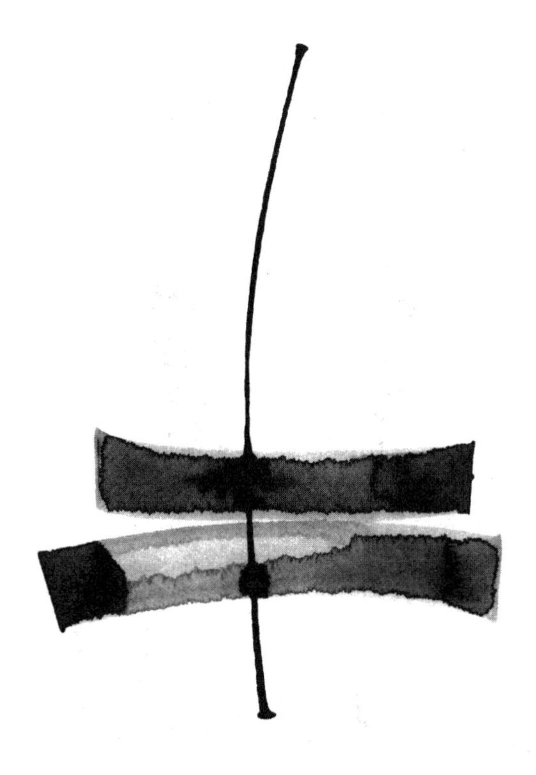

In the year's first frost
the late butterfly lies here
frozen in the grass.

LII

Gradu citato
equus stabulum petit:
vocant avenae.

At a full gallop
the horse hastes to the stable:
the oat is calling.

HVMANA

LIII

In her dainty hands
the small girl carries a loaf
as big as the sun.

LIV

Blue-green like the sea
are the lovely eyes of my
sweet little daughter.

LV

The son has come home;
he hears the kettle whistle
in his mum's kitchen.

LIII

Panem rotundum
pupa palmulis affert
magnum ceu solem.

LIV

Ut mare glaucum
est filiolae meae
dulcis ocellus.

LV

Filius redux
audit aquam ferventem
culina matris.

LVI

Manus leniter
ut eruca derepit
vibratque cutem.

Soft as a silkworm
the hand caresses the skin
making it quiver.

LVII

Aestate senem
involutum paenula
ductitat canis.

In summer time the
old man clad in a raincoat
follows his mongrel.

LVIII

Una cum luna
apparet de fenestra
dulcis amica.

At one with the moon
the beloved one appears
in my high window.

LIX

Sola vigilo
ad fenestram, nocturna
aura mulcente.

In my lonely watch
at the window I am touched
by the wind's caress.

LX

Iuxta me puer
fluctus irrequietos
observat gemens.

Next to me a boy
too watches the unquiet
waves, and sighs and sighs.

LXI

Puellam prodit
in angulo latentem
risus venustus.

The girl in hiding
in a corner is betrayed
by her sweet laughter.

LXII

Sursum deorsum
muliebria volant
pectora cursu.

Upward and downward
go the gently bouncing breasts
of women running.

LXIII

Boys and girls will kiss
hands and eyes and lips and mouths
frenetically.

LXIV

Oh if I could but
pluck you, Lycoris, blacker
than the mulberry.

LXV

The mirror used to
do her face, also serves to
observe the others.

LXIII

Iuvenes labris,
ulnis, oculis, ore
savia vorant.

LXIV

O te si carpam...
Nigrior es, Lycoris,
moro caduco.

LXV

Usa speculo
labra fuco dum linit
perlustrat omnes.

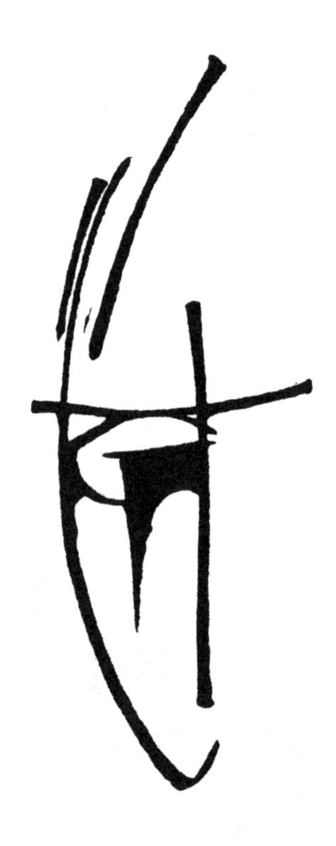

LXVI

Tristis puella
videt imbrem cadentem
turgidis guttis.

The melancholy
girl watches the rain falling
in thick heavy drops.

LXVII

Libasti labris
vix mea labra tuis,
blanda puella.

Your lips, my darling,
hardly touched mine although I
tried hard to kiss you.

LXVIII

Vitro madente
imbribus assiduis
exsequor pensum.

The window is full
of persisting black rainclouds;
I'll do my homework.

LXIX

Ludos amorum
pueri puellaeque
caute conantur.

Cautiously young men
and young women try out the
gentle plays of love.

LXX

Urbe relicta
muta per silentia
sonant campanae.

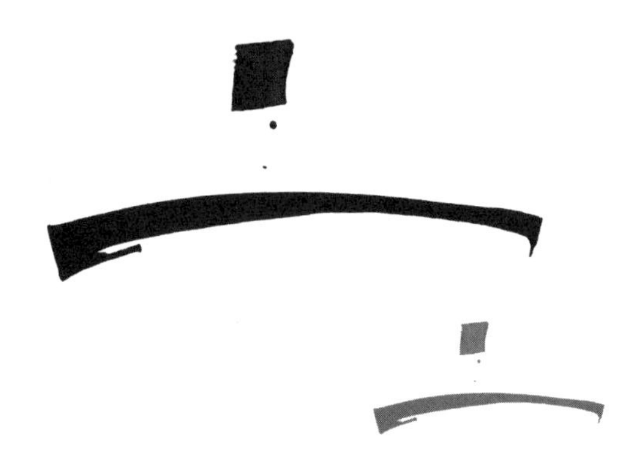

In the deserted
city no sound can be heard
but the sound of bells.

LXXI

Parvus thalamus
ubi tunc dormivimus
autumno pleni...

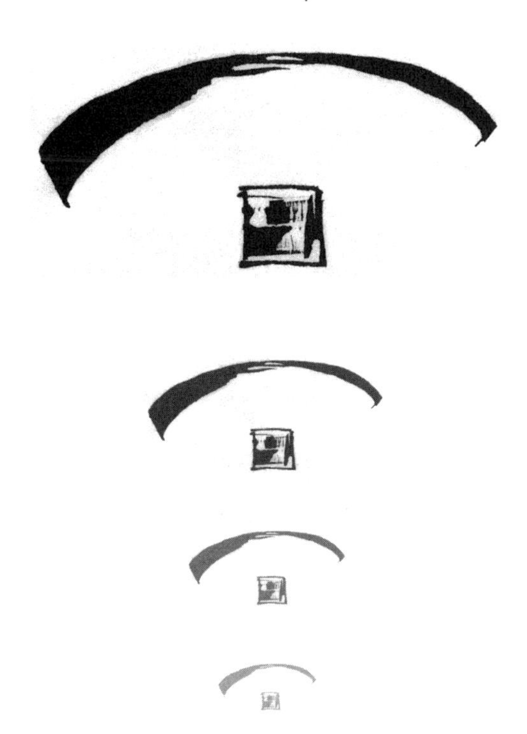

The small bedroom where
we spent the nights in those days
foretelling autumn.

LXXII

Lacrima tristis
temperata pluviis
genas perfundit.

A tear of sadness
mixes with a drop of rain
and runs down her face.

LXXIII

Mulier sola
audit Iovem tonantem
toto corpore.

A lonely woman
hears Jove's thunder resounding
in her very bones.

LXXIV

Nil attenta, nil
videns virgo praeterit
immemor mei.

Aware of nothing,
unseeing she walks past, not
remembering me.

LXXV

Haicu dum ludo
obrutus negotiis
repuerasco.

Overloaded with
care and work, I play Haiku,
and grow young again.

LXXVI

Tristitia
facit circulos
in piscina.

Sadness draws
circles
in the pool.

LXXVII

Fidibus canit
mundi solutus curis
amicus Musae.

The Muse's friend, he
plays the harp and all his cares
are dissipated.

LXXVIII

Amores penna
elegantior olim
nunc fessa scribit.

Her writing on love
that once was so elegant
is hackneyed and trite.

LXXIX

Obvius est mi
post ambulationem
odor cafeae.

Fragrance of coffee
coming to meet me after
my long morning walk.

LXXX

Agrestem Musam
harundine tenui
meditaberis.

You shall try out a
rural ditty on the thin
and pastoral flute.

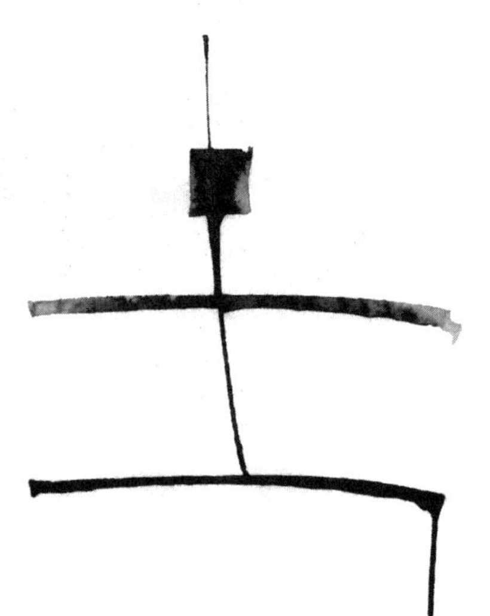

LXXXI

Immotus tenet
harundinem tremulam
pisces dum captat.

Motionless he holds
the trembling line and all the
while tries to catch fish.

LXXXII

Ut bellatrices
ad pretia remissa
tendunt matronae.

Like warriors all
the matrons rush to the shops
to buy cut price goods.

LXXXIII

Ad telephonum
mulier obdormivit;
murmurat imber.

At the telephone
the woman dozed off and the
rains keep murmuring.

LXXXIV

Tonight they all dance
the men and the women and
their shadows as well.

LXXXV

On a sunny day
the old woman closed the door
of her life, and left.

LXXXIV

Hac nocte saltant
viri mulieresque,
saltant et umbrae.

LXXXV

Aprico die
vita sua morosa
exit vetula.

LXXXVI

Primo calore
tugurii ianuam
aperit senex.

On the first warm day
the old one opens the door
of his gloomy hut.

LXXXVII

Nurum non aeque
tractant considerate
ac fictilia.

Her daughter-in-law
got less consideration
than her crockery.

LXXXVIII

Ruinas inter
vetula curva carpit
unum papaver.

Among the ruins
the old woman bends to pick
the only poppy.

LXXXIX

Moriturus sum;
inutiles in herbas
cadit pluvia.

I shall soon be dead;
the light rain falls steadily
on the useless herbs.

XC

Iam sunt recisae
obumbrantes sepulcrum
fagi vetustae.

They have all been felled,
the old beech trees which kept watch
over the graveyard.

XCI

Fumant fornaces,
filis aculeatis
insidunt corvi.

The ovens belch smoke;
the ravens on the barbed wire
are watching; they wait.

XCII

Salices inter
vetus latet sacellum,
latet ut Deus.

An ancient chapel
stands among trees, out of sight
and hidden like God.

Notes and Vocabulary

NOTES

CAELESTIA

I (Ramona Janssens - Har.)
vespertinus, -a, -um: of the evening
rutilare, -o, -avi, -atum: to have a reddish glow
nitor, -oris, m.: splendour

II (M.S. - A.W.)
Pleiades, Pleiadum, f.: the Pleiades (here with the Greek form of the accusative)
remotus, -a, -um: distant, remote

III (M.S.)
vitrum, -i, n.: glass
fluctuare, -o, -avi, -atum: undulate, fluctuate

IV (L.V.)
iners, -ers, -ers: inactive, inert, slow

V (Ryôkan - M.S.)
fenestrula, -ae, f.: little window

VI (A.V.)
virgula, -ae, f.: a little twig
nitor, -oris, m.: splendour (of the sun)
piceus, -a, -um: black as pitch

VII (M.S. - A.W.)
raeda, -ae, f.: carriage, car
nitescere, -o, nitui, -: to begin to shine or glitter

VIII (G.S. - D.S.)
rubescere, -o, rubui, -: to grow red
noctescere, -o, -, -: to grow dark

IX (D.S.)
reminiscent of Lucretius and Baudelaire
incanus, -a, -um: quite gray
operculum, -i, n.: cover
homuncio, -onis, m.: a little man

X (M.S.)
pedetemptim (adv.): step by step

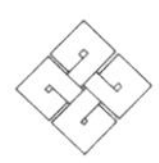

TERRESTRIA

XI (Santôka - M.S.)
aestuare, -o, -avi, -atum: to have a waving motion

XII (Sappho 2 C, 5–8 - A.V.)
stilla, -ae, f.: a drop
rorare, -o, -avi, -atum: to distil dew

XIII (Verg. Georg. I, 65–66 - M.S.)
gleba, -ae, f.: a clod
pulverulentus, -a, -um: full of dust
solibus = solis radiis

XIV (M.S.)
clavus, -i, m.: a nail

XV (D.S.)
emicare, -o, -ui, (-atum): to spring out

XVI (H.K.)
fagus, -i, f.: a beech
merula, -ae, f.: a blackbird, merle

XVII (Anon. - R.C.)
cogitabundus, -a, -um: thoughtful

XVIII (A.W.)
superbire, -io, (-ivi), (-itum): to be superb or splendid
aphaca, -ae, f.: a dandelion

XVIX (M.S.)
prunus, -i, f.: a plum-tree
scalae, -arum, f.: a ladder

XX (M.S.)
nymphaea, -ae, f.: a water lily

XXI (Catull. 11.22–24 - D.S.)
ilico (adv.): instantly

XXII (Catull. 11.22–24 - H.B.)

XXIII (M.S.)

XXIV (M.S.)
chamomilla, -ae, f.: a chamomile

XXV (Verg. Georg. I.85 - M.S.)
stipula, -ae, f.: a halm, stubble

XXVI (Petrarca, Bucolicum carmen 10.20–21 - D.S.)

ANIMALIA

XXVII (D.S.)
nidulus, -i, m.: a little nest
tepere, -eo, -, -: to be moderately warm or tepid,
  to glow with love
avicula, -ae, f.: a little bird
pipilare, -o, -avi, -atum: to cheep

XXVIII (Anon. - R.C.)
spatiari, -or, -atus sum: to walk about
ardea, -ae, f.: a heron

XXIX (Bashô - R.C.)
cicada, -ae, f.: a tree-cricket, cicada

XXX (Katja Leemans - Har.)
cavea, -ae, f.: a cage
mite (adv.): mildly, softly

XXXI (M.S.)
avicula, -ae, f.: a little bird

XXXII (Verg. Georg. 1.377 - M.S.)
stridere, -eo (-o), stridi, -: to make a creaking
  sound (with hirundo: martlet, swallow)

XXXIII (R.C.)
stipula, -ae, f.: a halm, a stalk (of corn)
ardea, -ae, f.: a heron

XXXIV (M.S.)
cuculus, -i, m.: a cuckoo
remotus, -a, -um: distant

XXXV (D.S.)
vitrum, -i, n.: glass, bowl
gyrare, -o, -avi, -atum: to turn around
pellucidulus, -a, -um: (almost) transparent, bright

XXXVI (G.S. - D.S.)
annosus, -a, -um: old
saltare, -o, -avi, -atum: to dance

XXXVII (Yasoko - R.C.)
catus, -i, m.: a male cat

XXXVIII (R.C.)
inhaerere, -eo, -si, -: to stick in
arcte (adv.): closely, firmly

XXXIX (D.S.)
prosilire, -io, -ui, -: to spring forth or up

XL (M.S. - A.W.)
adrepere, -o, -psi, -ptum: to creep slowly
glaucus, -a, -um: gleaming, grayish

XLI (L.V.)
an allusion to the eruption of Mt. Vesuvius in A.D. 79
canicula, -ae, f.: a little dog
pumex, -icis, m.: a pumice-stone; pumice-ash

XLII (L.V.)
asellus, -i, m.: a little ass
pulverare, -o, -avi, -atum: to bestrew with dust

XLIII (M.S.)
plangere, -o, -nxi, -nctum: to lament over

XLIV (Verg. Georg. I.379–380 - M.S.)
terere, -o, trivi, tritum: to rub (metaphorical, with iter: to tread repeatedly)
formica, -ae, f.: an ant

XLV (M.S.)
araneola, -ae, f.: a small spider
perspicillum, -i, n. (modern Latin): glasses

XLVI (Bashô - R.C.)

XLVII (M.S.)
xystus, -i, m.: a terrace
rana, -ae, f.: a toad

XLVIII (L.V.)
hircus, -i, m.: a buck
proterve (adv.): brutally, shamelessly
arietare, -o, -avi, -atum: to strike violently

XLIX (M.S.)
rugire, -io, -, -: to roar

L (M.S. - L.V.)
arrigere, -o, -rexi, -rectum: to set up, to erect

LI (Elske Everaerts - Har.)
papilio, -onis, m.: butterfly

LII (A.W.)
avena, -ae, f.: oat

HVMANA

LIII (M.S. - A.W.)
pupa, -ae, f.: a little girl
palmula, -ae, f.: a small palm of the hand
ceu (conj.): like

LIV (H.B.)
glaucus, -a, -um: grayish, sparkling

LV (M.S.)
culina, -ae, f.: a kitchen

LVI (Jurgen Peeters)
eruca, -ae, f.: a caterpillar
vibrare, -o, -avi, -atum: to set in tremulous motion
cutis, -is, f.: the skin

LVII (D.S.)
paenula, -ae, f.: a raincoat
ductitare, -o, -avi, -atum: to lead with one

LVIII (Jurgen Peeters - Har.)

LIX (H.B.)

LX (H.K.)

LXI (Hor. carm. I.9, 21–22 - A.V.)

LXII (D.S.)
sursum (adv.): upwards
deorsum (adv.): downwards

LXIII (D.S.)
ulna, -ae, f.: an elbow or arm
savium, -ii, n.: a kiss

LXIV (Mart. I.72, 5–6 - L.V.)
morum, -i, n.: a mulberry or blackberry
caducus, -a, -um: inclined to fall, overripe

LXV (D.S.)
speculum, -i, n.: a mirror
fucus, -i, m.: rouge
linere, -o, levi, litum: to spread over
perlustrare, -o, -avi, -atum: to assess with a glance

LXVI (Ellen Van Paesschen - Har.)
turgidus, -a, -um: swollen, turgid, tumid

LXVII (Janus Secundus, Basia 3.1–2 - L.V.)
libare, -o, -avi, -atum: to touch

LXVIII (Katja Leemans - Har.)
vitrum, -i, n.: glass, window
exsequi, -or, exsecutus sum: to carry out
pensum, -i, n.: homework

LXIX (Koen Steens)

LXX (Eef Cappelle - Har.)
campana, -ae, f.: a bell

LXXI (M.S.)

LXXII (Elske Everaerts)
temperare, -o, -avi, -atum: to mix

LXXIII (Yoshino - M.S.)

LXXIV (Bert Cappelle - Har.)

LXXV (D.S.)
obruere, -o, -rui, -rutum: to cover with or bury
repuerascere, o, -, -: to become a boy again

LXXVI (Kenshin - M.S.)
a free haiku in the style of the school of Seisensui
piscina, -ae, f.: fishpool

LXXVII (Elke Otten - Har.)
fides, -ium, f.: a lyre, stringed instrument

LXXVIII (An Michiels - Har.)

LXXIX (R.C.)
cafea, -ae, f. (modern Latin): coffee

LXXX (Verg. Ecl. 6.8 - M.S.)

LXXXI (Ovid. Met. 8.217 - A.V.)

LXXXII (Elke Otten - Har.)
bellatrix, -icis, f. (also adj.): a female warrior
pretium, -ii, n. (with remissum): bargain

LXXXIII (M.S.)
telephonum, -i, n. (modern Latin): a telephone
obdormiscere, -o, -ivi, -: to doze off

LXXXIV (Santôka -M.S.)

LXXXV (Nicolas Hibert - Har.)
apricus, -a, -um: sunny
morosus, -a, -um: dejected
vetula, -ae, f.: a little old woman

LXXXVI (M.S.)
tugurium, -ii, n.: a hut, cottage

LXXXVII (Akiyoshi - R.C.)
fictilis, -is, -e: earthen, fictile

LXXXVIII (A.W.)
vetula, -ae, f.: a little old woman

LXXXIX (Santôka - M.S.)

XC (D.S.)
obumbrare, -o, -avi, -atum: to overshadow

XCI (A.W.)
memory of Camp Majdanek (Poland)
fornax, -acis, f.: an oven
aculeatus, -a, -um: thorny, prickly

XCII (M.S. - A.W.)
salix, -icis, f.: a willow
sacellum, -i, n.: a chapel

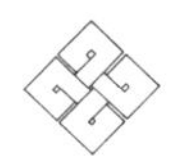

VOCABULARY

ac (conj.): and; in comparisons: than, as
accrescere, -o, -crevi, -cretum: increase, grow
aculeatus, -a, -um: prickly
ad (prep.): to, against, near, at, for
adrepere, -o, -repsi, -reptum: creep (into)
aeque (adv.): just as
aestas, -atis, f.: summer
aestuare, -o, -avi, -atum: be agitated
afferre, -o, attuli, allatum: bring, carry
agrestis, -is, -e: rustic
ambo, - ae, -o: both
ambulatio, -onis, f.: walk
amica, -ae, f.: friend
amicus, -i, m.: friend
amor, -oris, m.: love
angulus, -i, m.: corner
angustus, -a, -um: narrow
animal, -alis, n.: animal
annosus, -a, -um: aged
anxius, -a, -um: anxious, troubled
aperire, -io, aperui, apertum: open
aphaca, -ae, f.: dandelion
apparere, -eo, apparui, -: appear
apricus, -a, -um: sunny
aqua, -ae, f.: water
araneola, -ae, f.: small spider
aratrum, -i, n.: plough
arbor, -oris, f.: tree
arcte (adv.): closely, firmly
ardea, -ae, f.: heron
arietare, -o, -avi, -atum: butt, strike hard
arrigere, -o, -rexi, -rectum: raise
asellus, -i, m.: young or little ass
asinus, -i, m.: ass
assiduus, -a, -um: continual
attentus, -a, -um: attentive

audire, -io, -ivi, -itum: hear
aura, -ae, f.: breeze
auricula, -ae, f.: small ear
aurora, -ae, f.: dawn, morning
autumnus, -i, m.: autumn
avena, -ae, f.: oat
avicula, -ae, f.: small bird
avis, -is, f.: bird

bellatrix, -tricis, f.: warrioress
blandus, -a, -um: flattering, charming

cadere, -o, cecidi, casum: fall
caducus, -a, -um: inclined to fall, overripe
caelestis, -is, -e: of the sky
caelum, -i, n.: sky, heaven
cafea, -ae, f. (modern Latin): coffee
calor, -oris, m.: heat, warmth
campana, -ae, f.: bell
canere, -o, cecini, -: sing
canicula, -ae, f.: little dog
canis, -is, m./f.: dog
cantus, -us, m.: song, singing
captare, -o, -avi, -atum: try to catch
carpere, -o, carpsi, carptum: pluck, gather
catus, -i, m.: male cat
caute (adv.): cautiously, carefully
cautus, -a, -um: careful, cautious
cavea, -ae, f.: cage, hive
ceu (conj.): like
chamomilla, -ae, f.: chamomile
cicada, -ae, f.: tree-cricket, cicada
circulus, -i, m.: circle
circum (adv.): around
circumvolitare, -o, -avi, -atum: fly round
citatus, -a, -um: quick, impetuous
clavus, -i, m.: nail
coepisse, coepi, coeptum: have begun

cogitabundus, -a, -um: thoughtful
collis, -is, m.: hill
conari, -or, conatus sum: try
coniux, -iugis, m./f.: wife, husband, consort
considerate (adv.): cautiously
consumere, -o, -sumpsi, -sumptum: consume
coquere, -o, coxi, coctum: cook, bake
cornu, -us, n.: horn
corpus, -oris, n.: body
corvus, -i, m.: raven
cras (adv.): tomorrow
crepitare, -o, -avi, -atum: rattle, creak
cuculus, -i, m.: cuckoo
culina, -ae, f.: kitchen
cum (prep.): with
cunctus, -a, -um: the whole of, all
cura, -ae, f.: care, concern
cursus, -us, m.: running
curvus, -a, -um: curved, aged
cutis, -is, f.: skin

de (prep.): from, down from
decidere, -o, -cidi, -: fall down
decidere, -o, -cidi, -cisum: cut off
delabi, -or, delapsus sum: fall down, come down
demittere, -o, -misi, -missum: let down
densus, -a, -um: thick, dense
deorsum (adv.): downward
depre(he)ndere, -o, -ndi, -nsum: catch, intercept, surprise
derepere, -o, -repsi, -: creep down
deus, -i, m.: god
dicere, -o, dixi, dictum: say
dies, -ei, m./f.: day
diu (adv.): long, a long time
dolor, -oris, m.: pain, sorrow, trouble
dormire, -io, -ivi, -itum: sleep
ductitare, -o, -avi, -atum: lead on
dulcis, -is, -e: sweet, lovely, kind

dum (conj.): while
duo, -ae, -o: two

ecce (adv.): look!
efferre, -fero, extuli, elatum: bring out, carry out
ego, mei: I
elegans, -ans, -ans: elegant
emicare, -o, -cui, (-catum): dart out, shine
equus, -i, m.: horse
erigere, -o, -rexi, -rectum: raise up
eruca, -ae, f.: silkworm, caterpillar
esse, sum, fui, -: be
et (conj.): and
evanescere, -o, -nui, -: vanish, die away
ex / e (prep.): out of, from; down from
exire, -eo, -ii, -itum: go out, leave
exsequi, -uor, exsecutus sum: carry out

faber, -bri, m.: craftsman, smith
facere, -io, feci, factum: make, do
fagus, -i, f.: beech
feles, -is, f.: cat
fenestra, -ae, f.: window
fenestrula, -ae, f.: small window
fervere, -eo, ferbui, -: boil
fessus, -a, -um: tired
festinare, -o, -avi, -atum: hurry
fides, -ium, f.: lyre, harp
filiola, -ae, f.: little daughter
filius, -i, m.: son
filum, -i, n.: thread, string
flamma, -ae, f.: flame
flavus, -a, -um: yellow, golden
flos, -oris, m.: flower
fluctuare, -o, -avi, -atum: undulate, fluctuate
fluctus, -us, m.: wave, flood
flumen, -inis, n.: river
foedare, -o, -avi, -atum: mar, sully

folium, -i, n.: leaf
formica, -ae, f.: ant
fornax, -acis, f.: oven
fucus, -i, m.: rouge, red dye
fulgere, -eo, fulsi, -: flash, shine
fumare, -o, -avi, -atum: smoke
fur, -uris, m.: thief

gelu, -us, n.: frost, cold
gemere, -o, -mui, -mitum: sigh, moan
gena, -ae, f.: cheek
glaucus, -a, -um: bluish gray, green
gleba, -ae, f.: clod
gradus, -us, m.: step
gramen, -inis, n.: grass, herb
gutta, -ae, f.: drop, spot
gyrare, -o, -avi, -atum: turn around

haicu, -us, n. (modern Latin): haiku
harundo, -inis, f.: reed, cane, pipe, flute
herba, -ae, f.: grass, herb, weed
hic (adv.): here
hic, haec, hoc: this
hircus, -i, m.: buck
hirundo, -inis, f.: swallow
Hispaniensis, -is, -e: Spanish
homuncio, -onis, m.: little man, poor man
hortus, -i, m.: garden
humanus, -a, -um: human

iacere, -eo, -ui, -: lie, lie dead
iam (adv.): already
ianua, -ae, f.: door
ignis, -is, m.: fire
ilico (adv.): instantly, on the spot
ille, illa, illud: that one
imber, -bris, m.: rain, heavy shower
immemor, -or, -or: forgetful, negligent

immensus, -a, -um: immense
immotus, -a, -um: motionless, unmoved
in (prep.): in, on, at, into, towards
incanus, -a, -um: very gray
incurvatus, -a, -um: bent
iners, -ers, -ers: inactive, slow, inert
inhaerere, -eo, -haesi, -: hang in, stick in
insidere, -o, -sedi, -sessum: settle on, occupy
intellegere, -o, -lexi, -lectum: understand
inter (prep.): between, among, during
intra (prep.): inside, within
intrare, -o, -avi, -atum: enter
inutilis, -is, -e: useless
involvere, -o, -volvi, -volutum: envelop, wrap up
irrequietus, -a, -um: restless
iter, itineris, n.: way, march, road
iuvenis, -is, m./f.: young man, young woman
iuxta (prep.): near by, next to

labrum, -i, n.: lip
lacrima, -ae, f.: tear
lacus, -us, m.: lake
lascivus, -a, -um: playful, lustful, impudent
latere, -eo, -ui, -: to lie hidden, lurk
laurus, -i, f.: bay tree, laurel tree
lenis, -is, -e: soft, smooth, mild, gentle
leniter (adv.): softly, gently
lente (adv.): slowly
leo, -onis, m.: lion
lepus, -oris, m.: hare
levis, -is, -e: light
libare, -o, -avi, -atum: touch
linere, -o, levi, litum: smear, overlay
lucere, -eo, luxi, -: shine, be light
ludere, -o, lusi, lusum: play
ludus, -i, m.: play
luna, -ae, f.: moon
Lycoris, -idis, f.: Lycoris

madere, -eo, -ui, -: be wet, drenched
magnus, -a, -um: great, large, big
mane (adv.): in the morning
manus, -us, f.: hand
mare, -ris, n.: sea
mater, -tris, f.: mother
matrona, -ae, f.: married woman, lady
meditari, -or, meditatus sum: think over, practise
merula, -ae, f.: blackbird
meus, -a, -um: my
mille (indecl. in sing.): thousand
mirari, -or, miratus sum: wonder at, admire
miser, -sera, -serum: wretched, poor, pitiful
mite (adv.): mildly, cheerfully
modo (adv.): just now, a moment ago
mori, -ior, mortuus sum: die
morosus, -a, -um: difficult, dejected
mors, -ortis, f.: death
mortuus, -a, -um: dead
morum, -i, n.: mulberry
movere, -eo, movi, motum: move
mulcere, -eo, mulsi, mulsum: caress
muliebris, -bris, -bre: feminine, woman's
mulier, -eris, f.: woman, wife
mundus, -i, m.: world
murmur, -uris, n.: murmur
murmurare, -o, -avi, -atum: murmur, rumble
mus, muris, m./f.: mouse
Musa, -ae, f.: Muse
mutus, -a, -um: mute, silent

nebula, -ae, f.: mist, vapour
nebulosus, -a, -um: foggy, misty
nec, neque (conj.): and not, but not
negotium, -i, n.: business, work
nemus, -oris, n.: wood, grove
nidulus, -i, m.: little nest
niger, -gra, -grum: black

nihil / nil, nullius rei, n.: nothing
nimbus, -i, m.: cloud, rain
nitescere, -o, nitui, -: begin to shine, glitter
nitor, -oris, m.: splendour
noctescere, -o, -, -: grow dark
nocturnus, -a, -um: nocturnal
non (adv.): not
noscere, -o, novi, notum: get to know
nox, noctis, f.: night
nunc (adv.): now
nuper (adv.): recently, lately
nurus, -us, f.: daughter-in-law
nymphaea, -ae, f.: water lily

o (interj.): oh!
obdormiscere, -o, -mivi, -: doze off
oblivisci, -or, oblitus sum: forget
obruere, -o, obrui, obrutum: cover with, overload
observare, -o, -avi, -atum: watch
obumbrare, -o, -avi, -atum: shade, overshadow
obvius, -a, -um: in the way, to meet
Oceanus, -i, m.: Ocean
ocellus, -i, m.: eye, darling
October, -bris, -bre: of October
oculus, -i, m.: eye
odor, -oris, m.: smell, perfume
olim (adv.): once upon a time
oliva, -ae, f.: olive tree
omnis, -is, -e: all, every
operculum, -i, n.: cover
opprimere, -o, -pressi, -pressum: press down, overthrow
os, oris, n.: mouth, face
ovum, -i, n.: egg

paenula, -ae, f.: raincoat
palmula, -ae, f.: little hand
panis, -is, m.: bread
papaver, -eris, n.: poppy
papilio, -ionis, m.: butterfly

parvus, -a, -um: small
paululum (adv.): a little bit
pectus, -oris, n.: breast, heart
pedetemptim (adv.): step by step
pellucidulus, -a, -um: almost transparent, bright
penetrare, -o, -avi, -atum: penetrate, enter
penna, -ae, f.: feather, pen
pensum, -i, n.: homework
per (prep.): through, throughout
percipere, -io, -cepi, -ceptum: feel, understand
percutere, -io, -cussi, -cussum: beat, strike
perfundere, -o, -fudi, -fusum: besprinkle
perlustrare, -o, -avi, -atum: observe, survey
perspicillum, -i, n. (modern Latin): glasses
pes, pedis, m.: foot
petere, -o, -ivi, -itum: ask, go to
piceus, -a, -um: black as pitch
pipilare, -o, -avi, -atum: cheep, chirrup
piscina, -ae, f.: pool, fishpool
piscis, -is, m.: fish
plangere, -o, planxi, planctum: lament
Pleiades, -adum, f.: Pleiades
plenus, -a, -um: full
pluvia, -ae, f.: rain
polus, -i, m.: pole, sky
porta, -ae, f.: door
post (prep.): behind, after
praecedere, -o, -cessi, -cessum: go before, lead the way
praecludere, -o, -clusi, -clusum: shut
praeda, -ae, f.: booty, prey
praeterire, -eo, -ii, -itum: pass, go past
pratum, -i, n.: meadow
pretium, -i, n.: price
primus, -a, -um: first
procul (adv.): far
prodere, -o, -didi, -ditum: bring forth, betray
prope (prep.): near
prosilire, -io, -silui, -: jump up

proterve (adv.): brutally, shamelessly
prunus, -i, f.: plum tree
puella, -ae, f.: girl
puer, -eri, m.: boy
pulverare, -o, -avi, -atum: bestrew with dust
pulverulentus, -a, -um: dusty
pumex, -micis, m.: pumice-stone, pumice-ash
pupa, -ae, f.: little girl

quam (adv.): how, how much
quando (conj.): when
quasi (adv.): as if
-que (conj.): and
quies, -etis, f.: rest, peace, quiet
quietus, -a, -um: calm, peaceful, asleep

raeda, -ae, f.: carriage, car
ramus, -i, m.: branch
rana, -ae, f.: frog
recidere, -o, -cidi, -cisum: cut back, cut off
reddere, -o, -didi, -ditum: give back, make
redux, -ducis: brought back, returned
regyrare, -o, -avi, -atum: turn around again
relinquere, -o, -liqui, -lictum: leave
remittere, -o, -misi, -missum: send back, loosen, remit
remotus, -a, -um: distant, remote
repuerascere, -o, -, -: grow young again
restare, -o, -stiti, -: stand firm, remain
ripa, -ae, f.: river bank, shore
risus, -us, m.: laugh, laughter
rorare, -o, -avi, -atum: distil dew, drip
rosa, -ae, f.: rose
rotundus, -a, -um: round, circular
rubescere, -o, rubui, -: grow red
ruere, -o, rui, rutum: rush
rugire, -io, -, -: roar
ruina, -ae, f.: ruin, debris
rutilare, -o, -avi, -atum: have a reddish glow

sacellum, -i, n.: chapel
sacer, -cra, -crum: sacred
saevire, -io, -ii, -itum: rage
saevus, -a, -um: raging, cruel
salire, -io, -lui/-lii, saltum: leap, spring
salix, -icis, f.: willow
saltare, -o, -avi, -atum: dance
saltus, -us, m.: leap, bound
savium, -i, n.: kiss
scalae, -arum, f.: ladder
scopulus, -i, m.: rock
scribere, -o, scripsi, scriptum: write
sedere, -eo, sedi, sessum: sit
semper (adv.): always
senex, senis, m.: old man
sepulcrum, -i, n.: grave, tomb
serus, -a, -um: late
si (conj.): if
silentium, -i, n.: silence
silere, -eo, silui, -: be still, be silent
silescere, -o, -, -: calm down, fall silent
sol, solis, m.: sun
solus, -a, -um: alone, lonely, only
solvere, -o, solvi, solutum: loosen, release
sonare, -o, sonui, sonitum: sound
spatiari, -or, spatiatus sum: walk about
speculum, -i, n.: mirror
splendere, -eo, (splendui), -: be bright, shine
stabulum, -i, n.: stall, stable
stagnum, -i, n.: pool, swamp
stare, sto, steti, statum: stand
stella, -ae, f.: star
stilla, -ae, f.: drop
stipula, -ae, f.: halm, stubble
stridere, -eo (-o), stridi, -: creak
sub (prep.): under, beneath
superbire, -io, (-ivi), (-itum): be superb, be splendid
sursum (adv.): upward

suspendere, -o, -pendi, -pensum: hang up
suus, -a, -um: his, her, its, their

tamen (adv.): nevertheless
tandem (adv.): finally
tangere, -o, tetigi, tactum: touch, affect
tantum (adv.): only
tectum, -i, n.: roof
telephonum, -i, n. (modern Latin): telephone
temperare, -o, -avi, -atum: mix
tendere, -o, tetendi, tentum (tensum): proceed, go
tenere, -eo, tenui, tentum: hold, keep
tenuis, -is, -e: thin, fine, small
tepere, -eo, -, -: be lukewarm
terere, -o, trivi, tritum: rub, tread repeatedly
terra, -ae, f.: earth
terrere, -eo, terrui, -itum: frighten, terrify
terrestris, -is, -e: earthen, of the earth
thalamus, -i, m.: bedroom, marriage bed
tollere, -o, sustuli, sublatum: lift, raise
tonare, -o, tonui, -: thunder
totus, -a, -um: entire
tractare, -o, -avi, -atum: handle, treat
tremulus, -a, -um: trembling, shivering
tristis, -is, -e: sad, gloomy
tristitia, -ae, f.: sadness, melancholy, sorrow
truncus, -i, m.: trunk, bole
tu, tui: you
tugurium, -i, n.: hut
tunc (adv.): then
turgidus, -a, -um: swollen, distended
tuus, -a, -um: your

ubi (adv.): where
ulna, -ae, f.: elbow, arm
ultimus, -a, -um: farthest, the end of
umbra, -ae, f.: shadow

umere, -eo, -, -: be damp, be wet
una (adv.): together
unicus, -a, -um: one and only
unus, -a, -um: one
urbs, -bis, f.: city
urere, -o, ussi, ustum: burn
ut (adv.): as, just as
uti, utor, usus sum: use

vagus, -a, -um: wandering, unsettled, vague
velut (adv.): as, just as
venustus, -a, -um: charming, beautiful
verbum, -i, n.: word
vesper, -peri, m.: evening
vespertinus, -a, -um: of the evening
vetula, -ae, f.: old woman
vetus, -us, -us: old
vetustus, -a, -um: old, ancient
vibrare, -o, -avi, -atum: shake, set in tremulous motion
videre, -eo, vidi, visum: see
vigilare, -o, -avi, -atum: remain awake
virgo, -ginis, f.: maid
virgula, -ae, f.: small twig
vita, -ae, f.: life
vitrum, -i, n.: glass, bowl
vix (adv.): hardly, scarcely
vocare, -o, -avi, -atum: call
volare, -o, -avi, -atum: fly
vorare, -o, -avi, -atum: swallow, devour
vox, vocis, f.: voice, sound

xystus, -i, m.: walk, terrace

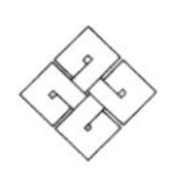

Bibliography

G. Immè, Haïcua cottidiana / Haïkaï quotidiens (Mazet St Voy, 1998)

B. Mesotten, Duizend kolibries. Haikoe van hier en elders (Sint-Denijs-Westrem, 1993) (including fifty Latin translations by A. Welkenhuysen, pp. 307–356)

W. Naumann, rec. H. Reinhardt, Haicua Latina (Freising, 1983), Zeitschrift der Deutschen Morgenländischen Gesellschaft, 136 (1986), 171–174

A.E. Radke, "Carmina, quae HAIKU more facta sunt. In hortum amoris," Vox Latina, 29 (1993), 389

———, In reliquiis Troiae. Auf den Trümmern Trojas. Lateinisch-deutsche Gedichte (Heidelberg, 1995) (pp. 14–15 and 60–61: Latin haikus with German translation)

———, Ars paedagogica. Erziehungskunst. Lateinische-deutsch. Gedichte und Prosatexte für Schüler Lehrer und Unterricht (Würzburg, 1998) (pp. 106–107: Latin haikus with German translation)

H. Reinhardt, Haicua Latina (private edition Freising, 1983) (with an epilogue "De conscribendis haicubus")

———, "Altera series haicuum," Hermes Americanus, 2 (1984), 87–89; "Tertia pars haicuum," ibid., 6 (1988), 120–122

———, Centuria haicuum. Das ist: Eine Sammlung von gut hundert Gedichten in japanischer Manier und lateinischer Sprache. Hrsg., übers. und kommentiert von von R. Chlada (Frankfurt/M., Bern, New York, Paris, 1991)

———, "Über das Haiku in lateinischer Sprache," Vierteljahresschrift der Deutschen Haiku-Gesellschaft, 4 (1991), Nr. 2, 11–16

———, "Haicua Vindobonensia," Rumor Varius, 86 (1991), 8–10

———, Angulus haicuum. Neue Dreizeiler in japanischer Art und lateinischer Sprache. Hrsg., übers. und kommentiert von R. Chlada (Fulda, [1993])

D. Sacré, "Ab oblivione vindicentur haicua Belgo-Latina," Melissa, 75 (1996), 8–9

———, "Haicua Latina," Rumor Varius, 118 (1997), 33

———, Harundine: Haicu dum ludo. Een bloemlezing van Latijnse haiku's (private edition Leuven, 1998)

M. Smets, "Latijn, een taal voor haikoe," Vuursteen, 7 (1987), 112–115

———, "Levende haikoe in een dode taal," ibid., 11 (1991), 120–122

———, "Haicua Latina. Een nieuwe lente en een nieuw geluid?," Kleio, 24 (1994-1995), 207–208

A. Welkenhuysen, "Latijn en haiku. Beschouwingen en voorbeelden," in id., Latijn van toen tot nu. Opstellen, vertalingen en teksten gebundeld naar aanleiding van zijn emeritaat. Redactie: W. Evenepoel, W. Verbeke, P. De Rynck, Symbolae, A, 18 (Leuven, 1995), pp. 149–158

———, "Latijnse teksten en verzen uitgekozen, ingeleid en toegelicht door D. Sacré," in id., pp. 339–393 (pp. 383–384: Latin translations of haikus of B. Mesotten; p. 385: Latin translations of haikus of M. Smets)

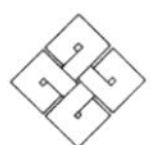